ROSE

A Production Manual

Gorakh Singh
Horticulture Commissioner
Department of Agriculture & Cooperation
Ministry of Agriculture, Government of India
Krishi Bhawan, New Delhi

K.V. Prasad
Senior Scientist
Division of Floriculture and Landscaping
IARI, New Delhi

T. Janakiram
Head
Division of Floriculture and Landscaping
IARI, New Delhi

WESTVILLE
WESTVILLE PUBLISHING HOUSE
New Delhi

Gorakh Singh, K.V. Prasad and T. Janakiram (2010), Rose — A Production Manual, 48p,
Westville Publishing House, New Delhi

First Published in 2010

978-81-85873-62-6

Published by Mrinal Goel, Westville Publishing House
47, B-5, Paschim Vihar, New Delhi – 110 063 (India)
Tel + 91-11-25284742, Fax: +91-11-25267469
Email: westville_2002@yahoo.co.in
Printed at Salasar Imaging Systems, New Delhi

ROSE

A PRODUCTION MANUAL

Rose, popularly known as the queen of flowers, is the single largest cut flower traded in the global market. The Government of India has identified the floriculture sector as one of the growth engines to fuel the economic growth with a great potential to earn the foreign exchange.

An ideal cut flower is one which has a long stems with glossy foliage, sturdy stalk with pointed flower buds that open slowly. The demand for cut flowers is increasing at the rate of 7-8 per cent per annum the world over and India is not an exception.

The cut flower production centres are located primarily in the southern and western parts of India owing to the favourable climatic conditions. Maharashtra, Karnataka, Andhra Pradesh, Haryana, Tamil Nadu, Rajasthan and West Bengal have emerged as major flower-growing states.

There has been a steady increase in cut flower production over the years (Table 1). The total production stands at 1,31,230 lakh cut flowers during 2009-10.

IDEAL ROSE SHOULD HAVE:

- long, strong and straight stems
- large flowers that open easily
- flowers with good colour and shape
- healthy leaves without symptoms of pests and diseases
- stems with short internodes
- maximum yield potential

Table 1. Cut flower production trend over the last five years

Year	*Number (lakh)*
2005-06	29,203.42
2006-07	37,158
2007-08	43,633
2008-09	1,13,618
2009-10	1,31,230

The production houses established in the northern India could not continue for a long period primarily because of extreme weather conditions prevailing in summer and winter seasons.

The total Indian export of floricultural products was Rs 340.14 crore during 2007-08 (Table 2) which was destined primarily to USA, Netherland, UK, Germany and Japan.

Table 2. Export of floricultural products from India

Year	*Quantity (tonnes)*	*Value (Rs, crore)*
2005-06	35,457.44	301.44
2006-07	42,545.28	652.69
2007-08	36,240.78	340.14

The Indian export basket comprises dry flowers (71%), fresh cut flowers (18%), live plants (9%), fresh bulbs (1%) and foliage (1%). Among fresh flowers exported from India, roses occupy a lion's share followed by other flowers.

Indian exports of cut flowers to the Europe stand at Euro 2.6 million (0.1% of the Euro 3 billion imports into the EU). Of which, 94% comprise rose imports. In terms of value, rose export from India stands at Euro 2.4 million (0.3% of total EU rose imports from outside the EU).

WHERE TO GROW?

Generally, rose can be grown everywhere in a protected environmental condition. The ideal location for rose growing should have a temperature range of 14 °C (minimum) to 28 °C (maximum), which is very commonly found around the equator and in the southern hemisphere.

In India, places like Bangaluru, Pune, Nashik, etc. with salubrious climate throughout the year, are most suitable locations both climatically as well as for infrastructure and logistics. The year-round mild climate in Pune and Bangaluru favours installation of cost-effective, naturally-ventilated greenhouses, thereby minimizing the cost per unit area.

On the other hand, locations with extreme summer (New Delhi and Hyderabad) dictate the use of both energy-intensive heating and cooling systems, thereby resulting in escalation of cost per unit area. Keeping the natural climatic advantage and cost-effective production technology in view, majority of the units have established state-of-the-art production systems in and around Bangaluru.

HOW DO WE GROW EXPORT QUALITY ROSES?

- By creating a microclimate — temperature, humidity and light for the plant
- Protection from rain and other weather elements
- Protection from pests and diseases
- Precise water and fertilizer management
- Intensive cultivation practices
- Proper harvest and post-harvest management

An ideal location should have:

- well-developed transportation system
- well-developed communication system
- efficient cold storage facility at airport
- well-connected flights to major national and international auction houses
- away from industrial pollution
- availability of both skilled and unskilled economical manpower
- availability of good quality water
- availability of uninterrupted power supply
- well-developed connecting road
- availability of various production inputs.

HOW TO SELECT A GREENHOUSE OR POLYHOUSE?

Intensive production of high-quality blooms, which satisfy the stringent export standards is very difficult in natural field conditions. Hence, protected cultivation in plastic covered greenhouses is absolutely essential for producing high-quality flowers. Considering economics of construction, a polyhouse is more suitable for Indian context compared to a glasshouse. Prevailing external climatic conditions of a locality dictate the type of greenhouse and other infrastructure to be installed for the production of roses.

It should be borne in mind that at least 2.5 °C temperature difference above ambient always

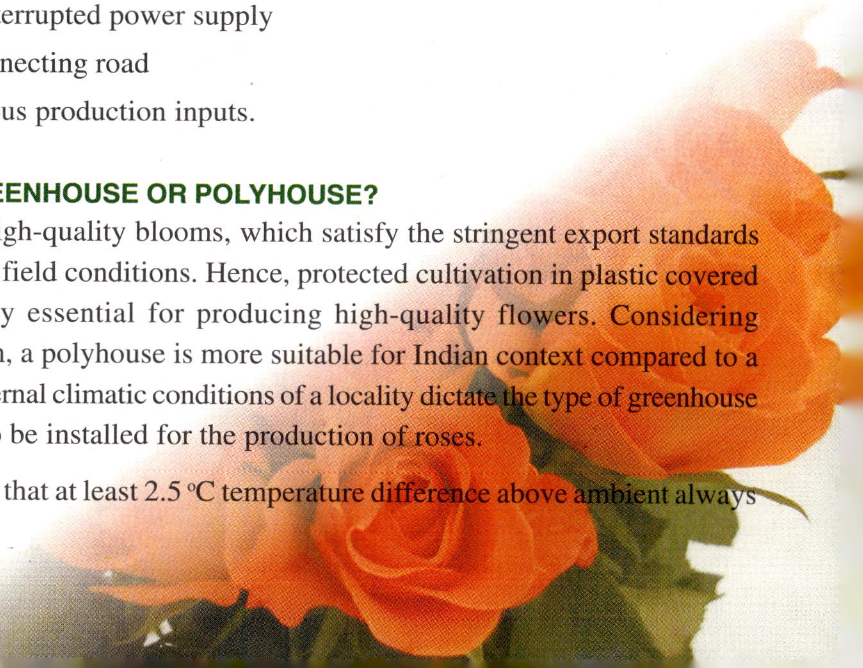

prevails in a polyhouse depending upon season and external environment. Therefore, cooling or heating systems have to be planned keeping in view the polyhouse temperature over and above the ambient temperature in different seasons.

WHICH SOIL IS IDEAL?

By nature, rose plants have deep-rooted and active feeding roots even at a depth of 50 cm, which imposes a heavy demand on the subsoil also. Hence, an ideal soil should be nutritionally rich, texturally loose and structurally stable down to a depth of about 50 cm having a pH of 5.5–6.0. Such soils ensure optimum drainage and aeration to its roots. Rose does not tolerate water-logging and high watertable. Therefore, an ideal soil must have a stable watertable well down the active root zone.

SOIL REQUIREMENT

- Natural soil is preferred over expensive soil-less media
- Sandy loams having a pH of 5.5–6.0
- 30% organic matter in top 30 cm soil
- Good drainage and aeration

Rose can also be grown in soil-less media like rock wool and peat-based substrates which are highly expensive. However, such alternatives can be considered only when soil has some inherent problem which cannot be resolved otherwise. In normal course, soil-based substrate fortified with locally-available organic derivatives like cocopeat can be economically used for commercial cultivation of roses.

How to Prepare Soil?

If soil has high salt concentration, it must be completely flushed with water by flooding the soil. Nearly, 400 litres of water for every one square meter of soil facilitates easy wash out of salts. Flooding the soil also gives an opportunity to test the drainage properties of the soil selected. The flooding of soil may be repeated for twice or thrice to leach out the salts completely. Such flooded soil is allowed to dry before ploughing is taken up. Preparation of soil in wet condition would harm its structural properties.

The soil must be ploughed to a depth of 40–50 cm without any compaction in between. Based on the soil test reports adequate organic manures should be incorporated into its soil to promote its structural properties. Organic-matter content of 10–12% by weight is optimum. The binding abilities for nutrients and water enhance in light soils by application of organic manures. Similarly in heavy soils, incorporation of organic matter enhances the much-needed aeration. FYM + Neem Cake + Paddy husk or coir pith may be added to the beds as per the requirement and availability to enrich the medium.

How to Ensure Drainage?

Appropriate drainage must be available at a depth of 40–100 cm for successful cultivation of roses. The number of drains and their placement depend on the type of beds to be laid and their orientation. The discharge installation such as pipes and ditches must be frequently checked to make sure the excess water is drained off quickly.

Soil pH

Roses perform very well when the soil reaction or pH is slightly acidic (6.2–6.8). At this range, the specific advantages include:

- the activity of soil microorganisms is at its peak. Which convert the complex organic and some insoluble fertilizers to water-soluble compounds, making them available to plants;
- at pH 6.2–6.8, the most needed macronutrients like nitrogen (N), phosphorus (P), potassium (K), calcium (Ca), magnesium (Mg) and sulphur (S) are available.

Why Soil Becomes Acidic?

The soil tends to become acidic due to formation of higher hydrogen ions by:

- decomposition of organic matter
- exchange of H^+ ions by plant roots to take up other nutrients
- chemical fertilizers mostly nitrogen fertilizer
- loss of bases like calcium, magnesium, potassium and sodium.

Therefore, it is advisable to use completely decomposed organic matter to prevent the formation of organic acids in soil.

Why Soil Becomes Alkaline?

The soil tend to become alkaline due to formation of OH^- ions or accumulation of salts comprising calcium, magnesium and sodium.

What will Happen if pH is High or Low?

- When the pH falls below 5.0 the micronutrients like aluminum, copper, boron, manganese and zinc are available in amounts that are toxic to plants. Beside, the soil becomes more compact and, therefore, less aeration to roots.
- When the soil pH approaches 8.0, the micronutrients such as iron, manganese, boron, copper and zinc become unavailable, whereas molybdenum is taken up in excess quantity.

How to Adjust Soil pH?

When the pH is below 6.0 or 5.5, it can be elevated by adding calcium carbonate or lime or calcium magnesium carbonate to the soil. The amount of lime needed depends on how low the pH is and also the soil type. If the soil contains higher amount of clay and organic matter, more quantity of lime is required to correct the pH. Similarly, if soil is light sandy, the lime required is relatively less. For instance, a typical loose sandy soil requires about 3.5 kg of lime for every 100 square feet of soil to raise the pH by 1 point. If the particle size of the lime is coarse, it takes more time to enhance the pH level. At the same time, the time required to rise the pH level is limited when finely ground fine lime is applied to soil.

In a situation where the pH levels are precariously acidic (4.0–4.5), such soils need to be corrected immediately by applying hydrated lime (or) slaked lime at the rate of 0.5 kg for every 30 square feet.

How to Adjust Alkalinity?

When the pH of the soil crosses 7.5 or 8.0, it can be lowered by applying wettable or superfine sulfur dust or gypsum or ferrous sulphate. When sulfur is applied, it is not advisable to use more than 0.5 kg for every 100 square feet of soil. Since, sulfur dioxide liberated from oxidized sulfur reacts with water to form a strong acid, i.e. sulfuric acid, damages the roots and plants. Similarly, when ferrous sulphate is used, it is advisable to use about 1 kg for every 100 square feet of soil to adjust the pH.

How to Sterilize Medium?

The native soil available in the selected location may be containing a high degree of microbial load which needs to be eradicated to prevent the incidence and rapid spread of pathogenic microorganisms. Therefore, soil sterilization using various strategies becomes essential for the successful cultivation of roses.

Solarization

Solarization involves complete covering of the soil with white polythene cover for 2-3 consecutive months during summer to generate enough heat in the soil to eradicate not only microbes but also some of the weeds (Fig. 1).

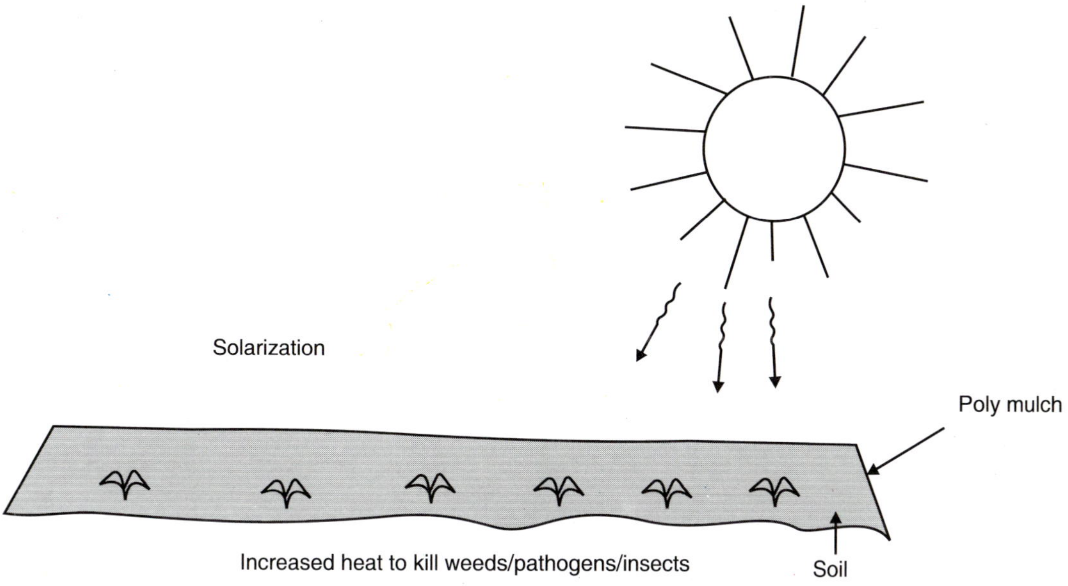

Fig. 1. Solarization for soil sterilization

Chemical Sterilization

Methyl bromide, chloropicrin and formaldehyde are the most commonly used chemicals for soil sterilization. Methyl bromide is normally mixed with 2% chloropicrin for easy detection in case of any accidental escape. The can containing methyl bromide under high pressure is placed in a special injecting device to deliver the liquid at appropriate depth which evaporates and liberates the toxic fumes. For every cubic meter of soil, 600 grams of methyl bromide is essential to sterilize the soil. The treated area is covered completely with polythene to prevent the escape of the gas, thereby making it more long-lasting in soil for effective control of microbes.

Chloropicrin, also known as 'tear gas', is also used as a sterilent through its soil penetration and spread is lower than methyl bromide just because it is not as toxic as methyl bromide. Usually, 32 ml of chloropicrin is injected for every square meter of soil through a mechanical injector.

Formaldehyde liberates highly toxic formalin which can be detected by its pungent odour and extremely irritating fumes. It can be applied either through soil injecting guns or by making feet deep pits at regular interval in the beds, pouring the formaldehyde solution and covering the pit with soil.

For all these sterilization methods, it is absolutely essential to cover the treated area with polythene covers to avoid the escape of toxic fumes. The treated area should be covered at least for 15 days without any disturbance in between. The treated polyhouses need to be ventilated slowly to facilitate human entry.

How to Organize Beds?

Depending on the soil type in polyhouse, the beds can be organized for growing roses. In case of heavy, poorly drained soils, the beds have to be raised at least up to 40 cm.

An optimum bed width of 1 m and a path width of 80 cm is ideal for Indian conditions and the length can be a continuous one without any break depending on the length of polyhouse, the beds can be of 20–40 m length (Fig. 2).

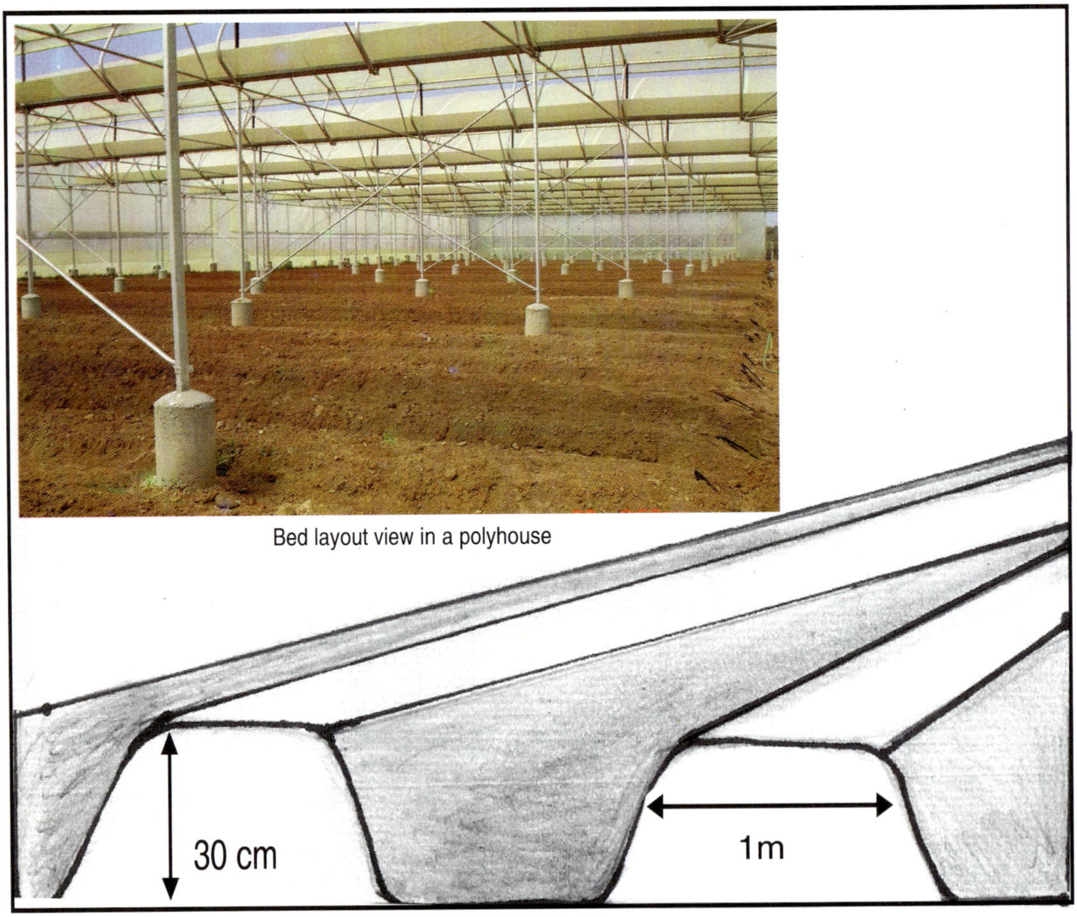

Bed layout view in a polyhouse

Fig. 2. Ideal bed size for planting roses

What to Plant?

In commerce, the cut stems of roses are classified as hybrid teas, floribunda, miniatures and sweet heart roses depending on nature and size of flowers besides stalk length.

Rose Varieties Grown in India for Export

The varietal preference keep changing in a fashion-driven industry like floriculture. Some of the varieties that are popular in India their production potential are enlisted hereunder. The world renowned breeders who have their representatives/local offices in India are summarised in Annexure III.

How to Plant?

A planting density of 7 plants per m^2 is ideal for remunerative yield of quality flowers. Therefore, in a polyhouse of 5,000 m^2, nearly 35,000 plants should be accommodated. In other countries, the plants are planted in 2–6 row system. As the number of rows increase, the operational difficulties like spraying, plant-protection measures, harvesting, building up of plants by pruning, etc. increase. Hence, for Indian conditions, 2-row system of planting is most ideal. Care should be exercised not to fold the roots in the planting pits. The planting pits should be deep enough to accommodate the root mass without folding and bending (Fig. 3).

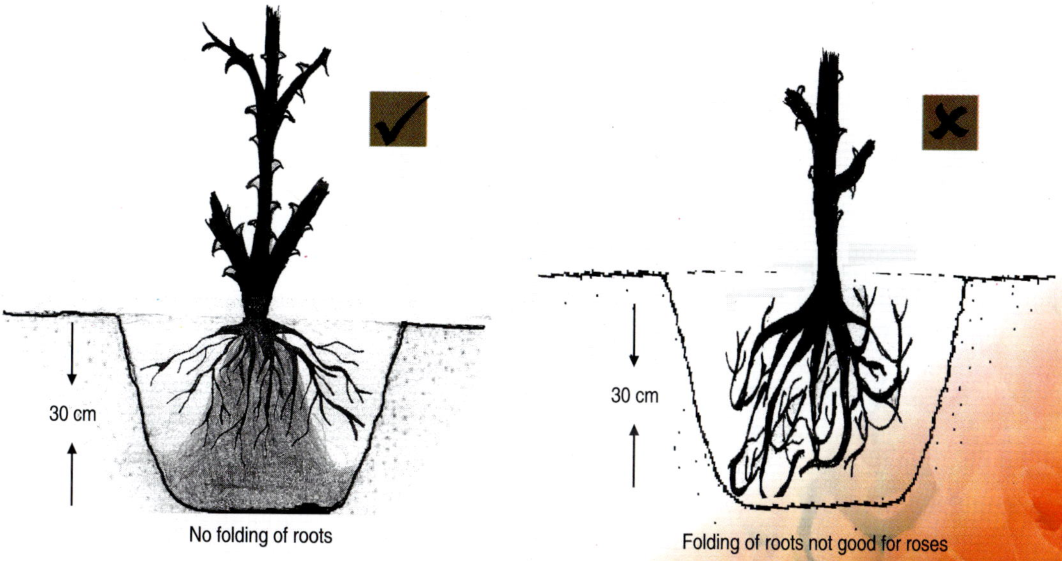

Fig. 3. Correct method of planting roses

Rose Varieties

Variety: **Carvette**
Flower colour: Pink
Flower size: Medium
Production: 180–200 stems/m^2
Av. stem length: 70–80 cm
Shelf-life: 10–12 days

Variety: **First Red**
Flower colour: Red
Flower size: Big
Production: 190 stems/m^2
Av. stem length: 80 cm
Shelf-life: 12 days

Variety: **Golden Gate**
Flower colour: Yellow
Flower size: Medium
Production: 300 stems/m^2
Av. dtem length: 50 cm
Shelf-life: 14 days

Variety: **Lambada**
Flower colour: Salmon
Flower size: Small
Production: 350 stems/m^2
Av. stem length: 55 cm
Shelf-life: 9 days

Variety: **Movie Star**
Flower colour: Pink
Flower size: Small
Production: 165–180 stems/m^2
Av. stem length: 60–75 cm
Shelf-life: 10–12 days

Variety: **Nobless-pink**
Flower colour: Pink
Flower size: Big
Production: 260 stems/m^2
Av. stem length: 60 cm
Shelf-life: 14 days

Variety: **Deyloa**
Flower colour: Mauve
Flower size: Big
Production: 160–180 stems/m^2
Av. stem length: 70–80 cm
Shelf-life: 11–12 days

Variety: **Gold Strike**
Flower colour: Yellow
Flower size: Medium
Production: 170–180 stems/m^2
Av. stem length: 70–80 cm
Shelf-life: 8–10 days

Variety: **Grand Gala**
Flower colour: Red
Flower size: Big
Production: 220 stems/m^2
Av. stem length: 65 cm
Shelf-life: 13 days

Variety: **Milva**
Flower colour: Pink:
Flower size: Large
Production: 180–200 stems/m^2
Av. stem length: 65–76 cm
Shelf-life: 10–12 days

Variety: **Narang**
Flower colour: Orange
Flower size: Medium
Production: 170–180 stems/m^2
Av. stem length: 65–75 cm
Shelf-life days

Variety: **Nobless-white**
Flower colour: White
Flower size: Medium
Production: 160–180 stems/m^2
Av. stem length: 60–80 cm
Shelf-life: 10–12 days

Variety: **Papilonia**
Flower colour: Yellow
Flower size: Medium
Production: 150–170 stems/m^2
Av. stem length: 60–70 cm
Shelf-life: 10–12 days

Variety: **Passion**
Flower colour: Red
Flower size: Medium
Production: 200–220 stems/m^2
Av. stem length: 50–60 cm
Shelf-life: 10–12 days

Variety: **Preety Women**
Flower colour: Pink
Flower size: Medium
Production: 150–170 stems/m^2
Av. stem length: 65–70 cm
Shelf-life: 10–12 days

Variety: **Priyanka**
Flower colour: White
Flower size: Medium
Production: 160–170 stems/m^2
Av. stem length 60–70 cm
Shelf-life: 10-11 days

Variety: **Ravel**
Flower colour: Pink
Flower size: Big
Production: 160 stems/m^2
Av. stem length: 90 cm
Shelf-life: 11 days

Variety: **Saphir**
Flower colour: Pink
Flower size: Big
Production: 160–180 stems/m^2
Av. stem length: 60–80 cm
Shelf-life 12–14 days

Variety: **Goldy**
Flower colour: Yellow
Flower size: Medium
Production: 220–300 stems/m^2
Av. stem length: 40–65 cm
Shelf-life: 15 days

Variety: **Skyline**
Flower colour: Light Yellow
Flower size: Medium
Production: 120 stems/m^2
Av. stem length (cm): 65–75
Shelf-life: 8–10 days

Variety: **Sweetness**
Flower colour: Pink
Flower size: Medium
Production: 160–180 stems/m^2
Av. stem length: 60–70 cm
Shelf-life: 10–12 days

Variety: **Tropical Amazon**
Flower colour: Ornage
Flower size: Small
Production: 155–165 stems/m^2
Av. stem length: 65–70 cm
Shelf-life: 8–10 days

Variety: **Versillia**
Flower colour: Cream
Flower size: Big
Production: 170 stems/m^2
Av.: stem length: 70 cm
Shelf-life: 11 days

Variety: **Yamma**
Flower colour: White
Flower size: Small
Production: 170–180 stems/m^2
Av. stem length: 55–65 cm
Shelf-life:10–12 days

Once the number of rows is decided, the plants can be planted at a distance of 18–30 cm depending on the nature of the variety. The long-stemmed varieties can be planted at 25-26 cm, while the short-stemmed at 18–25 cm (Fig. 4; Plates 1-4).

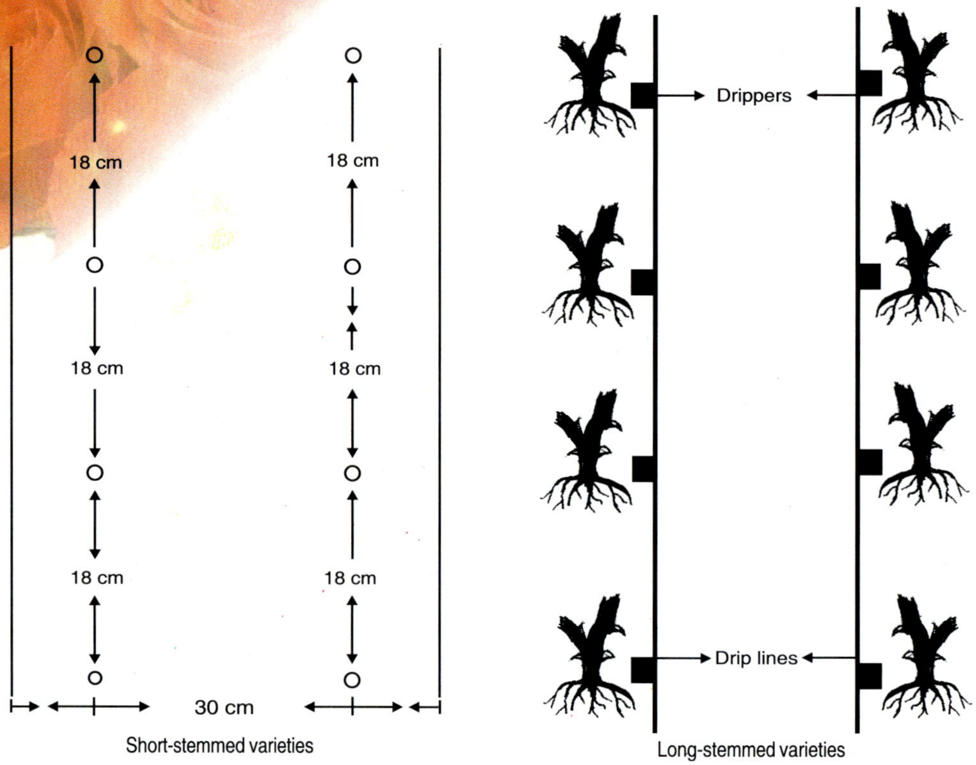

Fig. 4. Two-row planting system in rose

What Planting Material Should be Used?

Source: At present, the varieties suitable for protected cultivation are being imported from breeders' authorized suppliers from the Netherlands, Israel, France and Belgium. Research efforts are on in various ICAR research organizations like Indian Institute of Horticultural Research, Bangalore, and Indian Agricultural Research Institute, New Delhi, for evolving and selecting indigenous rose varieties suitable for export markets.

What is Royalty?

Since, the internationally acclaimed varieties are under intellectual property rights, royalty has to be paid to the breeders for any imported variety. At present, the royalty amount varies from Rs 40 to 50/plant. If royalty is not paid and the flowers are exported, the breeder has

Plate 1. Making of trenches for planting

Plate 2. Two-row planting in rose

Plate 3. Misting of newly-planted roses

Plate 4. Well-established plant population in a two-row system

all the rights to confiscate the consignment and proceed legally against the exporter. Exotic varieties developed by international breeders are also available in India, through authorized agents, who produce and sell them in India. A list of major authorized agents operating in India is summarized in Annexure III.

What Precautions are Needed while Importing Planting Material?

- The planting material should be produced from a reputed genuine propagator and supplier.
- Make sure that the planting material is free from insect pests.

- The planting material should especially be free from diseases like crown gal caused by *Agrobacterium tumefaciens.* It is imperative to recall that the Ecuador production in recent times plunged by 30% due to devastation by crown gall discasc alonc.
- Crown gall disease has already invaded some of the polyhouses in India to a limited extent. But it could become a major threat in future if its spread is not checked in the initial stages itself.
- Be vigilant and update knowledge on new pests and diseases which may be minor today but could explode to be a major threat in future if introduced inadvertently.

Which Type of Planting Material?

At present, the most popular types included plants on their own roots and those budded or grafted on a compatible rootstock. The plants with their own root system can be obtained either by producing rooted cuttings or by producing more number of rooted plants through by micropropagation.

What are Budded Plants?

The most commonly preferred type of rose plant material is the use of budded plants in the whole world. Dormant eyes on a scion (chosen variety) are budded either by T or inverted T or I method of budding on a rootstock. The rootstock plants are raised through cuttings and used for budding the scion bud wood by making a transverse cut followed by a vertical cut to lossen the bark for inserting the dormat bud (Plates 5-12). Most often the plants obtained from Europe are budded on *Rosa carnina* and *R. inermis*. The plants obtained from other tropical regions are mostly budded on *R. indica* or *R. manetti.* The plants obtained through budding take less time to build up and produce economic production in short time.

Plants budded or grafted on a rootstock are obtained by budding a dormant eye onto a specific rootstock (or) by joining the scion and the rootstock (Fig. 5). Some breeders also supply budded plants with a dormant eye inserted into a rooted stock. Such plants take relatively long time to build up and produce flowers.

How to Care after Arrival?

When rose bushes (i.e. traditional budded plants with 3-4 shoots of scion) are imported for planting the bushes are kept in water for 24 hours to replenish the water they lost during transit. They can be stored for a few days in cool protected place if planting is not taken up immediately. Such bushes must be protected from extreme temperature. If the planting is further delayed than expected then plant them very closely in a bed with proper covering of

Plate 5. Horizontal incision on rootstock

Plate 6. Vertical incision on rootstock

Plate 7. Dormant bud for insertion

Plate 8. Insertion of bud into 'T' section

Plate 9. Wrapping the bud with polyfilm

Plate 10. Successful sprout from scion

all the roots with soil. Apply a dose of systemic fungicide to prevent any disease attack.

When budded plants with dormant eyes are imported, the plants are kept in water for 24 hours as in previous case. Then the plants are planted closely in a bed and covered with a polyfilm to raise the temperature inside. At 18 °C, the buds sprout vigorously and once they reach pencil thickness the cover can be removed. Such a pre-treatment allows more uniform plant build up and uniform flowering in contrast to late flowering if the plants with dormant eyes are planted directly.

What Method of Planting?

Bushes: Dig pits to appropriate depth to accommodate all the roots without any bending. The long roots on the rootstock are lightly pruned and they are trained vertically into deep pits dig for planting them. The bud joint should be 5 cm above the soil surface. Care should be taken to ensure proper contact of roots with soil while filling the pits with soil. Do not compress the soil too much around the plant. Water the bushes to ensure proper contact and to remove air pockets, if any.

Plant with dormant eyes: Dig pits to appropriate depth to accommodate the roots with little bending, train the roots vertically and replace the soil. Ensure that the dormant bud is about two-and-a-half inches above the soil surface to prevent any rotting or fungal attack. If the dormant buds get submerged in soil the sprouting will be poor and might also result in decay.

Grafted plants: Pits are dig deep enough to train the roots vertically without any bending. Then replace the soil to ensure proper contact between the roots with the soil to facilitate

Plate 11. Successful budded plant in polybags

Plate 12. Excellent rooting of budded plants

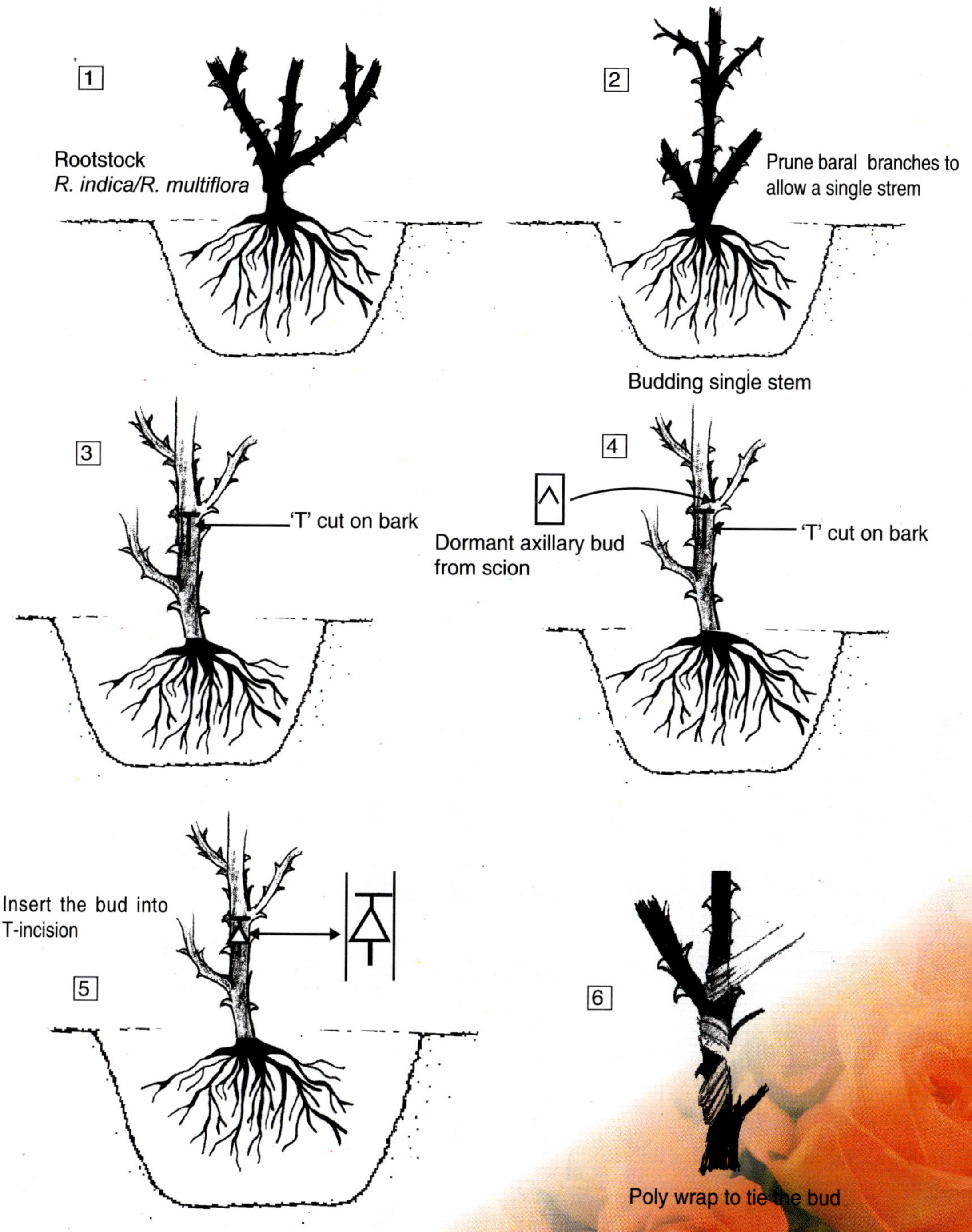

Fig. 5. Sequential steps in T-budding in rose

easy production of new roots. Ensure that the graft union is at least 2 inches above the soil surface to prevent fungal attack.

How to Care after Planting?

Bushes: The bushy budded plants are cut back to 10–15 cm after planting to prevent excessive water loss from the long stalks. Water frequently so that the roots are well-covered with soil and can absorb the water and nutrients. Spray a dose of systemic fungicide (carbendazim) to prevent any fungal attack.

Plant with dorment eyes: Ensure proper covering of roots as to raise the temperature to at least 18 °C to ensure proper sprouting. If the temperature falls below 10 °C the buds may not sprout. Remove the cover on cloudy days to prevent disease attack. Spray systemic fungicide to prevent disease attack.

How to Build up Plants?

Crop canopy management is a very important tool in commercial production of roses. If the young plants are allowed to flower immediately the entire structural framework of the plant is disturbed to a very great extent. Hence, developing an appropriate plant architecture is very essential by adopting various techniques.

The aim of building up of young plants must be to achieve a high performance production framework with appropriate amount of foliage as quick as possible. The crop canopy has to be developed in such a way that they harvest all the sunshine that reaches the ground in a polyhouse and convert them into assimilates through an efficient photosynthesis. The ratio between the aerial (shoots and leaves) and the submerged (roots) parts must be such that the roots provide enough water and nutrients to foliage and the foliage should provide enough assimilates to good framework of roots.

The plants can be built up by cutting, pinching, disbudding and pruning of roots which differ from different plant types obtained for planting.

How Environmental Factors Influence Growth and Development?

The growth and development of any crop is greatly influenced by the environmental regime available in the polyhouse and rose crop is not an exception.

How Temperature Influences?

Temperature influences to a greater extent to the growth and development of roses compared to other environmental factors. It is, therefore, crucial to rest the plants during winter and encourage new growth during other period with optimum temperature.

Best quality roses can be produced when the temperature hover around 28 °C during day and 18 °C during night. Such ideal temperature though difficult to maintain is essential to get the optimum growth and development. On the other hand, extreme temperature (either high or low) over and above optimum temperature would drastically affect the plant growth parameters enlisted in Table 3.

Table 3. Effect of temperature on roses

High temperature > 28 °C	*Optimum temperature 28 °C Day, 18 °C Night*	*Low temperature < 15 °C*
• Number of petals per flower get reduced at high temperature	• Increases the rate of development of plants	• The number of bull heads will be more
• The stem length gets reduced	• Efficient photosynthesis take place for maximum assimilate accumulation	• The numbers of blind shoots will be more
• The petals loose colour and look pale	• Enhanced flower yield per flush	• Darkening of petals. Some red coloured varieties appear almost black
• The length of the neck (thalamus) increases	• The flower quality of best	• Reduced growth rate and hence more time for production
• Drastically reduces the vase-life due to increase in respiration rate	• The overall health of the plant improves	• Vase-life gets reduced due to uptake of water

High temperature in a polyhouse can be managed by simple ventilation in places with mild climates (Bangaluru or Pune). Building up of high temperature can be checked by operating the shading system during bright sunny days in summer. If shading is done too often and for longer duration, though the quality of current season flowers would be good, the overall performance in subsequent years declines due to poor accumulation of photosynthesis in the plants. In extreme weather, places like Delhi, high temperatures can be managed by evaporative cooling from pad-and fan-system and microsprinklers (or) foggers (or) misters.

Low temperature especially during night is more detrimental to rose growth and flowering. The genetic programming of new sprouts to produce a flowering shoot or

IDEAL TEMPERATURE FOR ROSES

- Optimum day temperatures: 26–28 °C
- Optimum night temperatures: 15–17 °C
- Big variation between day and night temperatures not good
- Day 25–28 °C and night 18–20 °C ideal

VENTILATION

Ventilation is must to cool greenhouses
Ventilation requirement –

- AFR 0.04 cubic meter
- 1 air change/minute
- Air velocity 1m/s

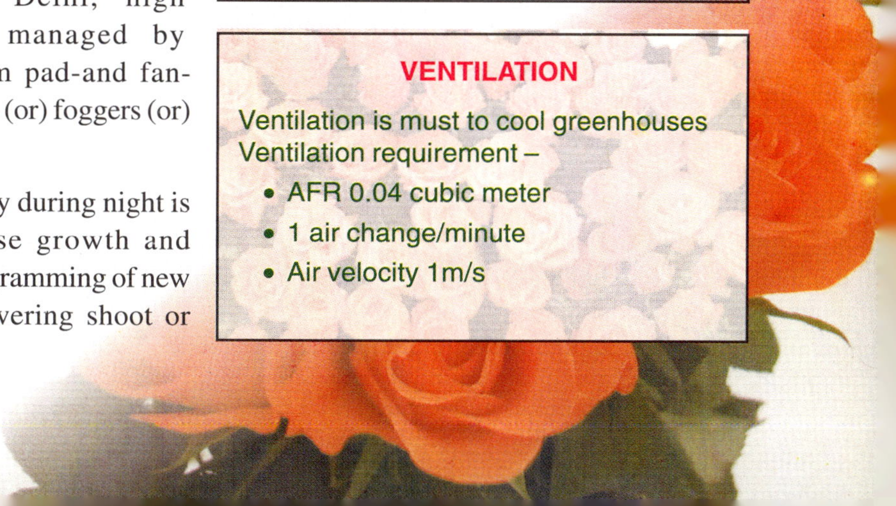

blind shoot happens early during their growth. Even if the shoots terminate into a flower bud, there is every tendency, that it can revert to vegetative phase (blind shoots) if exposed to low temperatures. The threat continues till the flower buds start enlarging and attain the size of a pea grain. Then the temperature can be reduced by 2-3 °C from 18 °C. Low temperatures during night also promote the attack of diseases especially when the diurnal variation is wide. Low temperatures beyond 10 °C in polyhouses, prompt the use of heating system (in places like Delhi and other places in northern plains) to raise the temperature levels to 15–18 °C.

Best quality roses are produced in tropical countries around equator, where the sunshine is in abundance. In temperate climates of northern hemisphere where the sunshine is low, to obtain equal quality blooms, nearly 6,000 lux of artificial lighting is essential. In India, where the sunshine is abundant, the need for costly artificial lighting is not recommended. The annual radiation (434 calories/cm^2/day) in Equador, where the world's best roses are produced, matches with many places in India, indicating the suitability for quality rose production.

How Relative Humidity Influences?

The monsoon season is of a particular concern for rose growing. Prolonged cloud cover, occasional showers and soaring relative humidity level which touch almost the saturation, are most congenial for incidence and outbreak of many diseases. Very high ambient humidity often results in condensation at low temperature and the resulting accumulation of water droplets on leaves and flower encourage the incidence of diseases like downey mildew and black spot. Excess humidity on the other hand can be regulated by operating the ventilation

LIGHT REQUIREMENT FOR ROSES

- Growth increases at 60,000 lux of light
- High light levels are required in winter
- Shading is required in summer: 35–50 per cent
- Shade nets or chalking the roofs are necessary to reduce light

TEMPERATURE CONTROL IN GREENHOUSE

It is controlled by:

- roof shading
- chalking the roofs and various combinations of white compounds
- shade nets (reflective, aluminized, saran or synthetic fibre)
- misting and hosing
- ground misting or overhead fogging
- hosing all exposed areas (evaporative cooling)

mechanism and operating heavy duty aerial fans to regulate the air flow terperature and humidity (Plate 13).

Humidity on the other hand, is quite essential for quality rose production. A moderate level of 50–60% humidity need to be maintained in polyhouses. Especially during hot summer months, besides operating mists/sprinklers the paths and other ground parts need to be kept moist in order to facilitate cooling as well as raising humidity levels in the microclimate.

Plate 13. Heavy duty aerial fan to regulate air flow, temperature and humidity

IRRIGATION

Water is the basic of supporting system in any living organism. Three basic questions, when to water?; how much to water? and how to water? – need to be raised before preparing an irrigation schedule for roses. Some of the important manufacturers of irrigation equipment are summarised in Annexure II.

> **WATER FOR ROSES**
>
> - use both borewell and rain water
> - adequate water throughout the year
> - quality of water needs to be checked well before planning
> - check water, particularly for sodium, chloride, bicarbonates and electrical conductivity

When to Water?

- marginal browning of leaves
- leaf drop
- rolled and curled leaves in some cultivars

- slight yellowing of leaves
- plants become too woody
- plant growth gets stunted
- foliage size gets reduced
- foliage is pale-green or dull grey-green in colour with absence of natural sheen and luster
- bent neck of flowers.

How Much to Water?

The quantum of water to be applied primarily depends on soil type in each polyhouse and the external environmental conditions.

DAILY WATER REQUIREMENT IN A WELL-DRAINED SOIL

Cold and cloudy	2 mm lost	2,000 litres/1,000 m^2
30% sunshine	3 mm lost	3,000 litres/1,000 m^2
60% sunshine	4 mm lost	4,000 litres/1,000 m^2
100% sunshine	5 mm lost	5,000 litres/1,000 m^2
Very hot and sunny	8 mm lost	8,000 litres/1,000 m^2

Water is absorbed from soil by the roots and lost by aerial foliage through a physical process called transpiration. Roses transpire much more water than they retain for their growth. The water requirement for roses depends primarily on the rate of transpiration and is often 500–1,000 grams of water for each gram of dry weight of plant. Besides transpiration, water is also lost by evaporation from the soil surface. The combination of water vapour loss from plant and soil is called evapotranspiration. The evaporation from an open pan evaporimeter acts as a guide to determine approximate amount of water to be applied as summarized in Table 4.

Table 4. Water requirement at different evaporation rates

Weather	*Evaporation losses (mm/day)*	*Water requirement* (*litres/1,000* m^2)
Cold and cloudy	2	2,000
30% sunshine	3	3,000
60% sunshine	4	4,000
100% sunshine	5	5,000
Very hot and sunny	8	8,000

Source: APEDA, New Delhi

How to Water?

The method of irrigating roses also depends on the soil type. The irrigation methods can be surface or subsurface types.

What is Surface Irrigation?

The traditional method of surface irrigation is by flooding the soil with hose pipes. Which is more detrimental than beneficial because of excess moisture, poor aeration, leaching of nutrients, etc. Recent surface irrigation systems are based on drip or sprinkling types. Through these systems water is applied slowly for one or more hours so that the entire growing medium can slowly absorb the water without flooding the soil surface. Water is distributed throughout the growing media by gravity and capillary action. The surface irrigation systems based on drip and sprinkler system can be automated by using solenoid valves and timers or electronic tensiometer control. The drip lines can be placed in between two rows and locating the drip nozzle exactly at the plant base. Similarly when a sprinkler system is used, the drip lines can be laid in centre of two rows and the sprinkling nozzle also in centre which rotates 360° and sprinkles on all surrounding plants.

Drip system of irrigation is more preferred because of more economisation of water and less build-up of relative humidity and the resulting disease outbreak. Sprinkler system is more advantageous in summer since it also aids in cooling the playhouses.

What is Subsurface Irrigation?

In this system of irrigation, the water is directly delivered at the root zone and, therefore, without much losses. In this system, the drip lines are placed in centre of two rows about 10–15 cm beneath the soil surface and the drip emitters are placed at the root zone. This method can also be atomized by solenoid valves and timers or electronic tensiometer system.

What Quality of Water?

Before finalizing the irrigation schedule, it is prerequisite to test the quality of water which directly influences the plant growth. The physio-chemical properties of water presented in Table 5 provide an overall view of various constituents, their suitability levels for optimum growth and development. Ideal water quality should be such that the range of various constituents should fall in optimum or low range. However, finding such ideal location with suitable water quality is quite seldom. However, some of the parameters can be easily manipulated by resorting to correction methods (Table 6).

Table 5. Quality of irrigation water

Chemical property		*Relative hazard*				
	Unit	*None*	*Little*	*Moderate*	*High*	*Severe*
When expressed in millequivalents/litre						
Bicarbonates	me/l	< 2	2-3	3-4	4-6	> 6
Chloride	me/l	< 4	–	4–6	6–10	> 10
Sodium	me/l	< 3	–	3–9	–	> 9
When expressed as parts per million (milligram/litre of water)						
Bicarbonates	ppm	< 122	122-183	183–244	244–366	> 366
Chloride	ppm	< 144	–	144–216	216–360	> 360
Sodium	ppm	< 69	–	69–207	–	> 207
Lithium	ppm	< 25	–	–	–	–
Zinc	ppm	< 2	–	–	-	–
Iron	ppm	< 1	–	–	–	–
Manganese	ppm	< 1	–	–	–	–
Fluoride	ppm	< 1	–	–	–	–
Boron	ppm	< 0.3	03-0.5	0.5-1.0	1.0-2.0	> 3.0
Copper	ppm	< 0.2	–	–	–	–
Electrical conductivity	dS/m	0.2	< 0.7	0.7-2.0	2.0-3.0	> 3.0
Sodium adsorption ratio	No unit	< 3.0	3.0-6.0	6.0-8.0	8.0-9.0	9.0

Table 6. Comprehensive evaluation of water

Critical parameter	*Evaluation*	*Prediction*
Total anions and cations	Anions: Chloride (Cl^-) Sulfates (SO^{4-}) Carbonates (CO^-_3) Bicarbonates (HCO^{3-}) Nitrates (NO_3^-) Phosphates (PO_4^-) Cations: Calcium (Ca^{2+}) Magnesium (Mg^{2+}) Sodium (Na^{2+}) Ammonium (NH^{2+}_4) Potassium (K^+)	The milliequivalents of anions should be equal to milliequivalents of cations
Calcium and magnesium	Concentration of calcium and magnesium	Determines whether water is hard or soft. Might cause scaling on leaves by deposition of Ca, Mg carbonates. Can clog the drip lines.

(*Contd.*)

Critical parameter	*Evaluation*	*Prediction*
Carbonates bicarbonates	Concentration of carbonate (CO_3-) and bicarbonates (HCO_3-) compared to bicarbonates.	Predicts level of alkalinity. Influence of carbonates is less on alkalinity when bicarbonate content must be < 3 meq/ln (183 ppm).
Macronutrients	Ammonium (NH_4^+) Nitrate (NO_3-) Phosphorous (P) Potassium (K)	If present in higher concentration it aids in reducing the fertilizers doses to that extent.
Micronutrients	Copper (Cu) Zinc (Zn) Manganese (Mn) Iron (Fe) Boron (B)	If Fe, Mn are more than 1 ppm, they might precipitate and cause rusty patches on foliage when sprayed. Manganese deposits in metal pipes and valves might hinder operation. If Boron is < 0.3 ppm, water needs supplemental dose to correct the deficiency and if > 1.5 ppm causes toxicity.
Electrical conductivity	Measure of salinity or salt content	If the EC is high the irrigation frequency and quantum of irrigation need to be increased to flush out excess salts.
pH	Measure of H^+ OH^- ion concentration on a negative logarithm scale	Denotes acidity or alkalinity of water.

How to Enrich Roses?

The most important aspect in greenhouse cultivation of roses is nutrition. The fertilizer regime is followed only after the soil and water analysis is carried out and the quantities are compared with the standards available. It is always desired that the nutrients are applied in smaller quantities at more frequency so that the plants get a regular supply of the required nutrients.

Commercial grade 100% water-soluble or liquid fertilizers are used to enrich the roses that are usually given through irrigation system (fertigation).

FERTILIZER SOLUTION FOR ROSES

$NO_3 - N$	156 mg/litre	P	46 mg/litre
Ca	132 mg/litre	K	174 mg/litre
$S\text{-}SO_4$	23 mg/litre	Fe	1.5 mg/litre
Mn	1.1 mg/litre	B	0.28 mg/litre
Mo	0.003 mg/litre	Cu	0.15 mg/litre

If the water has a very low EC then the above solution will have an EC of about 1.7 mS/cm

TARGET VALUES IN SOIL

NH_3	2.9 mmol/litre	K	1.1 mmol/litre
NH_4	0.1 mmol/litre	Na	1.0 mmol/litre
SO_4	1.1 mmol/litre	Ca	1.4 mmol/litre
HCO_3	0.5 mmol/litre	Mg	0.8 mmol/litre
P	0.14 mmol/litre	Zn	1.0 µmol/litre
Fe	7.0 µmol/litre	B	7.0 µmol/litre
Mn	0.18 µmol/litre	Cu	0.8 µmol/litre

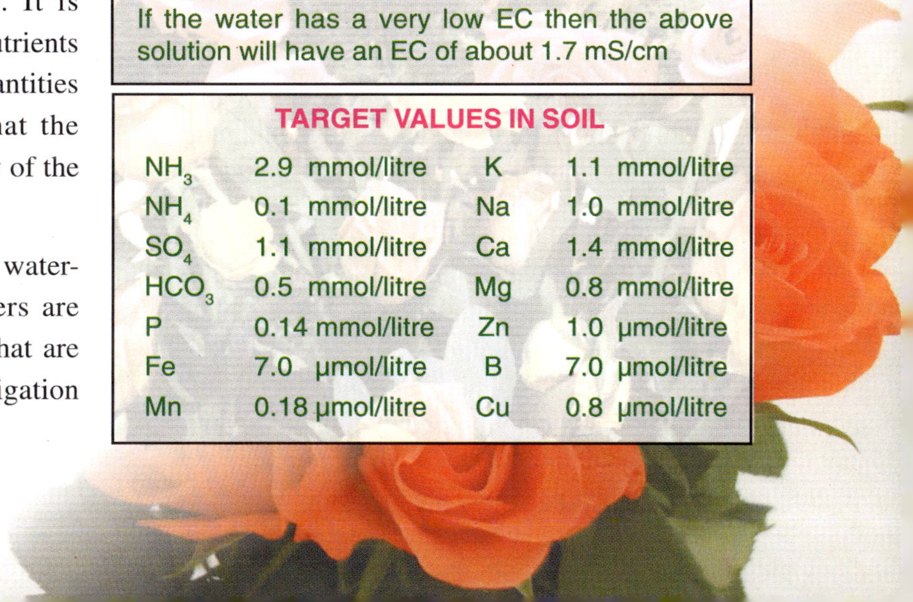

In order to ensure the maximum availability of all the nutrients, it is advisable to maintain a soil pH of 5.5 and 6.3. When grown under poly-house conditions rose is a heavy feeder, especially on nitrogen and potassium; moderate feeder on phosphorus, magnesium, sulphur, manganese, copper and molybdenum. It is very sensitive to iron and boron deficiencies.

PRODUCTION PROBLEMS

- Temperature, light and humidity
- Greenhouse architecture
- Water and fertilizer management
- Planting material
- Varieties of rose
- Rootstock used
- Pests and diseases

To avoid precipitation of sparingly-soluble salts such as calcium, phosphate or sulfate, two separate tanks are (A and B) installed. Tank A contains calcium-based salts, while Tank B consists of the remaining nutrients. A third tank containing acid for pH control is often installed.

The recommended concentration of nutrients in fertigation solution for roses is as follows:

Nutrient	Concentration (milli moles/litre)	Nutrient	Concentration (micro moles/litre)
NO_3	10.5	Fe	35.00
H_2PO_4	1.50	Mn	20.00
SO_4	0.75	Zn	2.50
NH_4	0.25	B	20.00
K	5.75	Cu	0.50
Ca	3.00	Mo	0.50
Mg	0.75		

The concentration indicated in the above table is indicative and needs to be adjusted in tune with the soil and leaf analysis values. During summer months, the nutrient requirement of roses per unit area per day is distributed into three equal parts and is injected into the drip lines when irrigated in the morning, afternoon and evening. Whereas during rainy and winter seasons, the frequency of irrigation is reduced and the nutrient content is adjusted into one or two irrigations. Some of the important manufacturers of fertilizers is enlisted in Annexure IV.

TROUBLE-SHOOTING IN ROSES

Like other crops, roses also pass through many hurdles that are of biotic and abiotic in nature. The crop could face problems due to poor management or environment-induced stresses.

HOW TO MANAGE INSECT PEST IN ROSE?

The important insect pests, their symptoms and control measures are summarized in this section. A list comprising important pesticide manufacturers is annexed at Annexure V.

Sucking Pest

Aphids

Symptoms: The aphids attack the tender parts, tips and young flowers. Infestation is more on shoot tips and young flowers. Both the nymphs and adults suck sap and reduce vigour of the plants.

Management: Spraying of 0.05% Monocrotophos or 0.02% Phosphomidon or 0.1% Malathion or 0.03% Dimethioate at 10–15 days interval effectively controls the aphids. Spraying of 1% neem oil also helps in control.

Thrips

Thrips *(Scirtothrips dorsalis)* is a serious problem on roses grown in polyhouses almost round the year except during November–December and July–August (Plates 14 and 15).

Symptoms: Both nymphs and adults suck sap from tender leaves, growing buds and flowers. Curled leaves with brown streaks, scorched appearance of sepals and petals of growing buds and deformed flowers with burnt margins are the main symptoms.

Management: Spraying of Insecticides like imidacloprin 20% SL 0.4 ml/litre or Cartap hydrochloride (50 SP) 1.5 g/litre or Fipronil (5 SC) 1 ml/litre or Acephate (75 SP) 1.5 g/litre at 10–15 days interval based on level of infestation checks thrips damage effectively. Drenching beds after raking up with Chlorphyriphos (20 EC) 4 ml/litre reduce-resting (pupal) population. Spraying of *Jatropha curacas* or *Pongamia glabra* oils 10 ml/litre followed by water extracts of *Calotropis giganted* or *Pedilanthus thithymaloides* leaf extracts at 100 g/litre before or after insecticidal sprays is effective in reducing thrips population.

Spider Mite

Two spotted spider mite (*Tetranychus urticae*): The mite is found initially in colonies two lateral black spot feed on leaves (Plate 16).

Symptoms: Discoloration, bronzing and drying of leaves. Cobweb formation of young branches, damage to buds and flowers lead to discoloration, retardation and drying (Plate 17-19).

Management: Cutting and burning of severely infested plant parts, proper ventilation and watering to reduce temperatures keeps the pest under control in polyhouses. Spraying of Abamectin (1.9 EC) 0.5 ml/litre or Milbemectin (1% EC) 0.5 ml/litre followed by

Plate 14. Thrips damage on flower buds

Plate 15. Thrips damage on fully-developed buds

Plate 16. Mite damage on young shoots

Plate 17. Mite damage on young buds

Flufenoxuron (10 DC) 1 ml/litre or Fenazaquine (10 EC) 1 ml/or Difenthiuron (50 SC) 0.6 ml/litre sprays combat mite problem. Also spray Dicofol (18.5 EC) 2.5 ml/litre or wettable sulphur (80 WP) 3g/litre or Profenofos (50 EC) 1ml/litre or Ethion (50 EC) 1ml/litre followed by pongamia or neem or jatropha oil at 5 ml/litre during off-season. Release of predatory mite *(Amblyseius tetranychivorus)* at 20 mites/plant when *T. urticae* population is at moderate level is also effective. Spraying of *Verticillium lecanii* formulation at 5 g/litre during evening provides considerable control.

Plate 18. Mite damage on unfurling buds

Plate 19. Mite damage on fully-developed flowers

Red Scales

Symptoms: The reddish-brown projection noticed on older shoots is an indication of the incidence and attack. The scales are mostly stationary and start sucking sap from plants. The affected plants lose vigour and present a sticky appearance.

Management: Clean cultivation and destroying affected plant parts prevent further multiplication and spread. Spraying either contact or systemic insecticides offers good control of scales. Spray (0.05%) Monocrotophos or Methyl parathion or Chloropyriphos or Dimethioate for early control of scales.

Whitefly (*Bemisia tabaci*)

The pest is active during January–July under protected conditions. Small and fragile white adults lay eggs on lower surface of young leaves (Plate 20).

Symptoms: The nymphs and adults suck sap mostly on the lower side of the leaf. The leaves crinkle and appear yellow and finally dry.

Management: Spraying of Diclorvos (76 EC) 1 ml/litre followed by Lambda chalothrin (5 EC) 1 ml/litre or Deltamethrin (2.8 EC) 1 ml/litre at 5–7 days interval is very effective. Installing yellow sticky traps check adult population. Triazophos (40 EC) 1.5 g/litre alternating with Pongamia oil 10 ml/litre at 15 days interval provides good control to whitefly.

Plate 20. Whitefly damage in rose

Bud caterpillar (*Spodoptera litura*)

Eggs are laid in groups on lower surface of leaves and damage is seen throughout monsoon period in polyhouses (Plate 21).

Symptoms: Early instars are gregarious in nature and feed on leaves by scraping chlorophyll. Black coloured mature larvae damage growing buds and flowers mainly by feeding during night resulting in considerable yield losses.

Plate 21. Bud caterpillar damage in rose

Management: Collection and destruction of egg masses and leaves infested with early instar larvae prevents pest build up. Spraying of Quinalphos (25 EC) 2 ml/litre or Methyl parathion (50 EC) 1 ml/litre or Endosulphan (35 EC) 2 ml/litre 15 days interval provides effective control. New compounds (75 WP)1g/litre are highly effective in controlling the pest in case of heavy infestations. Application of spodoptera NPV @ 250 LE/hour followed by neem formulations 1-2 ml/litre is also effective in checking larval population. Spreading of poison bait made of wheat/rice bran, jaggary and Chlorpyriphos (10:1:0.5) effectively kills grown-up larvae. Proclaim (Ememactin Benzoate) @ 5% WG (0.05 gm/lit) is very effective in controlling the caterpillars.

HOW TO MANAGE DISEASES IN ROSE?

The important diseases, their symptoms and control measures are summarized in this section.

Powdery Mildew (*Podosphaera pannaosa*)

Powdery mildew (*Podosphaera pannaosa*) is the most important disease on roses grown in both greenhouses and in the open. Favoured by warm and dry weather and widely varying day and night temperatures, the fungus grows well at 18–25 °C. Under field conditions night temperature of 15.5 °C and relative humidity of 90–99% promote optimum production of its conidia and their germination.

Symptoms: Greyish-white powdery patches are seen on tender leaves, pedicels and flower buds. Younger leaves of 7–10 days old are more susceptible than older ones. Infected leaves get malformed and flower buds fail to open and plants show wilted appearance (Plate 22 and 23).

Plates 22 and 23. Powdery mildew in rose

Management: Many contact and systemic fungicides are Carbendazim (Bavistin 0.1 %), Myclobutanil (systhane 0.05%) etc. Among the more recent compounds, two strobilurins, viz. kresoxym methyl and azoxystrobin which are surface systemic protectants are effective in controlling powdery mildew. Sodium bicarbonate offers good control of powdery mildew and also black spot. Some inorganic salts namely, di-potassium hydrogen orthophosphate and potassium dihydrogen orthophosphate (4.5 g/litre) control powdery mildew very effectively. Foliar spraying of these salts give better control compared to fungicides. Besides, some Antitranspirants namely polyterpenes and hydrocarbon wax emulsions are also effective in controlling of powdery mildew. The cultural practices that keep the disease under control include minimization of nitrogenous fertilizers and irrigation through sprinkler misters. Among the bioagents, two antagonistic fungi namely, *Ampelomyces quisqualis* and *Psuedozyma floculosa,* can control powdery mildew when their spore suspensions are sprayed on foliage.

Die Back

Die back (*Diplodia rosarum, Collectotrichum* sp. etc) generally occurs after pruning. The infection occurs at the pruned ends of stems or through wounds caused due to harvesting of flowers and other operations. Old plants are more prone to die back (Plates 24 and 25).

Symptoms: The infected stems dry from tip downwards, often extending to the main stem and thus killing the entire plant. Browning and rotting of infected stem extends inside the stem even beyond the infected lesions on the stem surface. Plants defoliated due to black spot and downy mildew are more susceptible because of depletion of carbohydrates in stems. Pruning the infected stems 5–10 cm below the margin of infection and pasting the pruned ends with Bordeaux mixture or rose paint (copper carbonate and red lead, Pb304) and linseed oil at a 4:4:5 ratio or Carbendazim (Bavistin 0.1%) give effective control of the disease. To avoid digger wasp damage any of the common insecticides may be mixed with these fungicides. While pruning, a slant cut is advised in order to avoid formation of water droplet on the out ends.

Plate 24. Initial entry of die back on pruned shoots

Plate 25. Die back disease in rose

Downy Mildew

Unlike in other crops affected by downy mildew *(Peronospora sparsa)*, the external symptoms are not clearly visible in the early stages of the disease on rose.

Symptoms: Downy mildew is very common on greenhouse roses because of the prevalence of high humidity and low temperatures. Initially the symptoms appear as pinkish-brown, irregular spots on tender leaves. The fungus causes chlorotic blotches on the upper surface of matured leaves, which ultimately become necrotic. The infection result in total defoliation and severe flower blight. The infected flowers get malformed and fail to open. Relative humidity of above 85% and temperature around 18 °C are optimal for multiplication of this fungus.

Management: The disease can be successfully brought under control by spraying of Fosetyl-Al (Aliette 0.3%), Metalaxyl-MZ (Ridomil-MZ 0.2%) or Cymoxanil (cuzate-M 0.2%).

Reducing the humidity in polyhouses effectively checks the spread of the disease. In nurseries, overcrowding of plants should be avoided by providing enough space among them.

Grey Mold

Symptoms: The infection of grey mold (*Bortytis cinerea*) is generally seen on inner whorls of petals. In favourable conditions, the infection spreads very fast, resulting in complete blighting of flowers. Humid and wet conditions in greenhouses favour the growth and multiplication of the fungus. A temperature range of 10–25 °C and a relative humidity of above 85% are highly favourable for disease development.

Management: Botrytis had developed resistance to all the important groups of fungicides that were effectively used earlier. Chemicals with anti-senescent activity render the plants more tolerant. Application of growth regulators like gibberellic acid, paclobutrazol and methyl jasmonate suppresses grey mold in roses. Inhibitors of ethylene biosynthesis such as amino-oxyacetic acid, carbon dioxide also reduce grey mold in roses. Since *Botrytis* sporulates readily on wounded and senescent tissues, these should be thoroughly removed from the greenhouses and destroyed. Biological agents like *Gliocladium roseum, Myrothecium verrucaria, Trichoderma harzianum* and *Penicillium* spp. are effective in controlling grey mold.

Crown Gall

Crown gall (*Agrobacterium tumefaciens*) is the most important disease of rose nurseries in many countries. About 20% of nursery stock is destroyed due to crown gall every year. The infection gradually decreases the vigour and yield of its plants.

Symptoms: Cauliflower like galls are produced most commonly at the crown region of the stem at the ground level. Galls are also formed on roots and on stems wounded due to harvesting, pruning and other cultural operations. The bacterium can move systemically in the plant and can survive as latent infection. Agrobacterium is a gram negative, soil-borne bacterium having a worldwide occurrence. The bacterium has a very wide host range. Earlier, it was believed to be pathogenic only to dicots. Now, it is known to affect about 60% of gymnosperms and dicot angiosperms besides Arales and Liliales among the monocots. Recently, this has become a major problem on roses in India. This bacterium requires moist wounds for infection.

Management: Clean nursery practices and production of disease-free planting material are prerequisites for its management. Remove and destroy all infected plants. Root damage by *Meloidogyne incognita* increases the incidence of crown gall. Hence, care should be taken to prevent nematode infestation of rootstocks. As rose genotypes, namely *Rosa indica, R. multiflora, R. canina* and *R. manetti* vary widely in their tolerance to crown gall, most tolerant among them may be used for rootstocks in order to limit the spread of the disease

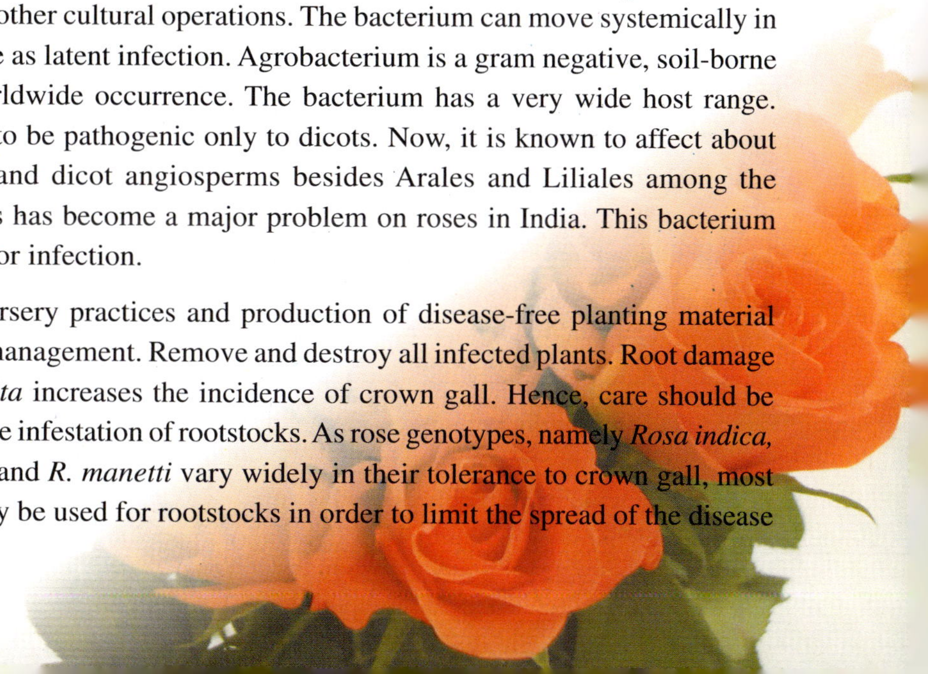

as the rootstock is the main target of attack by *Agrobacterium*. A very efficient biocontrol strategy is available against crown gall. A non-tumorigenic strain of *Agrobacterium radiobacter* (strain-K-84) is being successfully used in many countries to control crown gall.

POST-HARVEST MANAGEMENT OF ROSES

When to Harvest?

For distant markets, cut the flowers when the sepals start unfurling and buds become tight. However, they are cut when one or two petals unfurl for local markets.

Harvest roses between 8:00 and 10:00 AM and sometimes as early as 6:00 AM, if there is enough daylight. The hotter the weather, the earlier one should cut the roses. It is advised to irrigate the rose beds the night before harvesting so that flowers are turgid.

Use a sharp and clean cutter, and cut the rose stems at an angle so that water does not stay at the cut ends, which favours the entry of microbes. Re-cut the rose stems under the water to eliminate air bubbles, which can decrease flower life and promote premature wilting of the rose bloom.

Do We Need to Cut Under Water?

The cut ends of the flowers need to be put in clean chlorinated water immediately after harvesting so that the air does not enter the conducting tissue. Air lock in the conducting tissue hampers the water uptake and thereby the vase-life.

Why to Pre-cool?

Pre-cooling is an important operation done immediately after harvesting to remove the field heat. It is done in a cool chamber at 2–4 °C so that the flowers rapidly loose the heat acquired by them in the field/greenhouse.

What Sanitation Levels to be Maintained?

All the buckets and other containers need to be thoroughly washed with clean chlorinated water to prevent the spread of microorganisms from consignment to consignment. The processing halls need to be cleaned regularly so that the microbial load is minimum in the processing area. All the tools and implements used for the processing need to be wiped with absolute alcohol to ensure microbe-free status.

Where to Store?

In order to reduce the respiration rate and carbohydrate depletion in the cut flowers the flowers need to be stored at low temperature. At lower temperature the flowers produce less ethylene and sensitivity to ethylene also decreases at low temperature storage. Lower temperature also retards the water loss and development of microorganisms, thereby improving the quality of cut flowers. Roses are stored normally at 4.0 °C when stored in wet-condition, whereas they are stored at 0-1 °C when they are stored in dry condition.

Rehydration

The ability of the cut flowers to rehydrate in shortest span of time determines the post-harvest quality of cut flowers. Therefore, utmost care is essential to prevent clogging of the conducting vessels of the cut stems. The clogging can be prevented by dipping the cut ends in water immediately after harvesting and also after every re-cut at various stages of processing.

How to Grade Flowers?

The rose stems are graded as per the stem length. The demand for longer stem roses is more in Russia and East European markets. Whereas the short-stemmed roses are more preferred in the Japanese market. The flowers are graded in a grading hall (Plate 26) using grading boards (Plate 27) and are packed in two rows (Plate 28).

Stem length (cm)	*Grade*
> 80	A
60-80	B
40-60	C
< 40	D

Floral Preservatives

Floral preservatives extend the life of cut roses. Floral life, is one of the commercial products added to the vase water to enhance the vase-life of flowers. Chrysal is a different type of preservative used for keeping cut roses stored under refrigeration for several days before making bouquets.

How to Pack Roses?

The packing of flowers varies from country-to-country. For export to Europe and Japan: singles in 20s, sprays in 10s have to be packed. For United States, flowers in groups of 25s are packed. The flowers are wrapped at the head portion with corrugated sleeves to protect bloom from bruising (Plate 29). Bunches should be secured to prevent slipping by using rubber bands. A standard 20 volume/kg box holds 300–400 long-stemmed roses and up to 800 short-stemmed roses.

How to Transport?

The cut flowers destined for domestic and export markets are normally transported by air

Plate 26. Grading hall

Plate 27. Grading board

Plate 28. Flowers for two-row bundle making

Plate 29. Flowers wrapped in corrugated sleeves

cargo. Usually in the Indian domestic flower market, the flowers are often transported by train or roadways. Very often most of the flowers are shipped without refrigeration, which reduces their shelf-life. Refrigerated van containers are generally used to transport cut roses meant for the export. These vans transport the produce from the production centre to the airport and to the concerned markets after reaching the destined airports.

ECONOMICS OF ROSE CULTIVATION

Area	:	1 ha
Plant population	:	72,000 plants
Cost of planting material @ ₹50/plant (including royalty)	:	₹ 36,00,000 for 5 years, ₹ 7,20,000/year
Variety mix	:	Red (80%) : Others (20%)
Flower production	:	12,60,000/ha (126 flowers/m^2)

Operational expenses	*Cost (Rs)*
Manures and fertilizers	3,48,009
Pesticides	2,01,679
Labour	5,37,811
Marketing costs	3,04,760
Amortized fixed costs	4,41,453
Packing, transportation, logistics	2,63,083
Miscellaneous	1,44,088
Total	**22,40,883**
Returns	
Flower production/ha	12,60,000
Domestic sales	27,21,600
Export returns	3,02,400
Gross returns	30,24,000
Net returns (gross returns—operational expenses)	7,83,116
Benefit: cost ratio	**1:1.35**

QUALITY STANDARDS FOR CUT ROSES FOR EUROPEAN UNION

The quality standards prescribed for the export to European Union as prescribed by the European Commission are furnished here.

Definition of Produce

This standard shall apply to fresh unifloral stems of varieties (cultivars) of the genus Rosa of kind suitable for bouquets or for decorative purposes.

Provisions Concerning Quality

The purpose of this standard is to define the quality requirements of fresh cut roses at the dispatching state, after preparation and packaging.

Minimum Requirements

The roses must have been carefully harvested and have reached a stage of growth, which allow them to open properly. In all classes, subject to the tolerances allowed, the cut flowers must be:

- whole (although signs of disbudding and removal of leaves and thorns from the lower third of the stem are permitted, provided they do not affect the commercial appearance or presentation)
- fresh
- normally formed

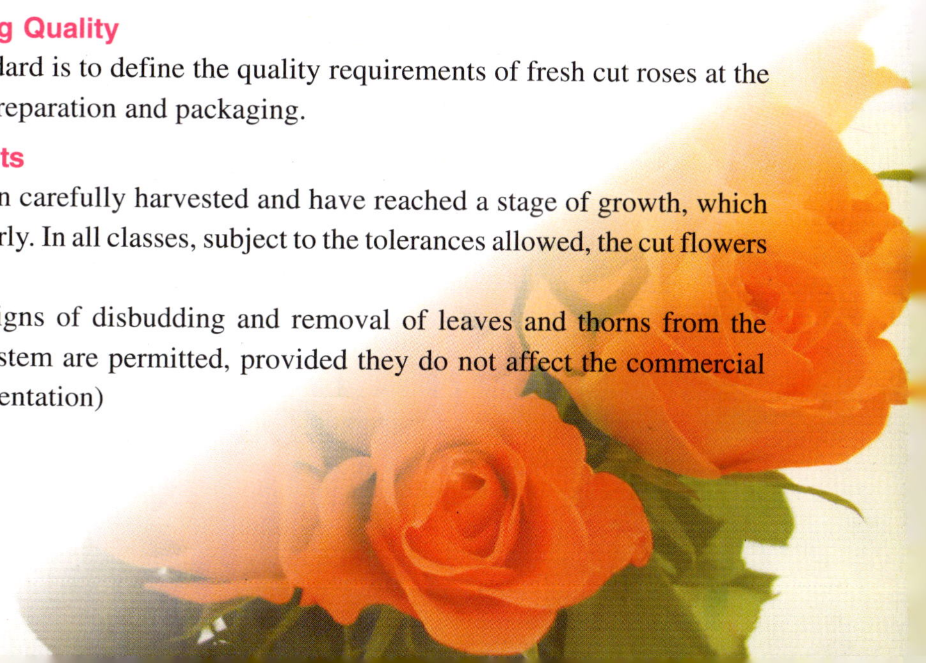

- free of animal parasites
- free of frost damage
- free of obviously "chlorotic" leaves.

The stems must be free of wood remaining from a previous year's growth. The development and condition of cut flowers must be such as to enable them to withstand transport and handling, and to ensure that they arrive in satisfactory condition at the place of destination.

Classification

Cut roses are classified into three classes, as defined below:

Extra class: Cut roses must be of superior quality. They must have the characteristics of the species and of the variety (cultivar).

Standard H-3: All parts of the cut flowers must be:

- free of damages caused by parasities of animal or vegetable origin
- free of visible extraneous matter affecting the appearance
- free of bruising
- free of defects of development
- Stems must be straight, rigid, strong and single, with healthy leaves.

(ii) *Class I*

Cut roses in this class must be of good quality. They must have the characteristics of the species and of the variety (cultivar).

All parts of the cut flowers must be:

- practically free of damages caused by parasites of animal or vegetable origin
- practically free of visible extraneous matter affecting the appearance
- practically free of defects of development
- practically free of bruising
- stems must be rigid, practically straight, sufficiently strong and single, with healthy leaves.

(iii) *Class II*

This class comprises cut roses, which do not qualify for inclusion in higher classes but satisfy the minimum requirement specified above. The cut flowers and parts of flowers may have the following defects:

- slight damage caused, for example, by diseases, parasites, treatment products, etc.
- slight visible traces of extraneous matter
- sligt bruising or deterioration, such as may be caused by frost
- slight malformation that does not prevent them from opening
- The stems may be less rigid, less strong, less straight, but not twisted. The defects permitted must not impair the keeping quality, appearance or utility of the products.

Provisions Concerning Sizing

For cut flowers, sizing must comply at least with the following scale:

Code	*Length (cm)*
5	5–10
10	10–15
15	15–20
20	20–30
30	30–40
40	40–50
50	50–60
60	60–80
80	80–100
100	100–120
120	More than 120

These lengths include the flower head. The difference per unit of presentation (bunch, bouquet, box and the like) between maximum and minimum length of flowers in the unit may not exceed:

- 2.5 cm for flowers in codes 15 and below
- 5 cm for flowers in codes 20 and 50 inclusive
- 10 cm for flowers in codes 60 and above.

Provisions Concerning Tolerances

The following tolerances in respect of quality and size are allowed for produce not satisfying the requirements of a particular class.

Quality Tolerance

Quality tolerance shall be permitted in each unit of presentation (bunch, bouquet, box and the like) as follows:

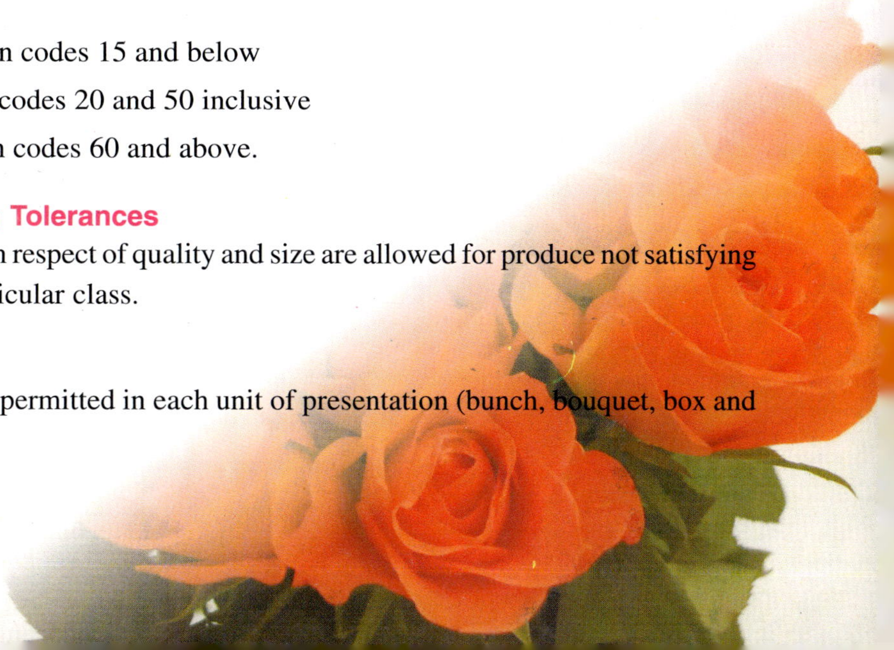

(i) *Extra Class*

Three per cent of the cut flowers, by number, may have slight defects, on condition that the uniformity of flowers in a unit of presentation is not affected.

(ii) *Class I*

Five per cent of cut flowers, by number, may have slight defects, on condition that the uniformity of flowers in a unit of presentation is not affected.

(iii) *Class II*

Ten per cent of the cut flowers, by number, may vary from the requirements of the class. Half of this percentage may have been attacked by parasites of animal or vegetable origin. The defects in question must not impair the utility of the products.

Size Tolerance

Size tolerance shall be permitted in each unit of presentation as follows: In all classes, 10 per cent of the cut flowers may vary from the length requirement of the sizing code.

Provisions Concerning Presentation

Uniformity: Each unit of presentation (bunch, bouquet, box and the life) must contain flowers of the same genus, species or variety (cultivar) and of the same quality class, and must have reached a uniform stage of development, with the exception of Class II. Mixtures of flowers or mixtures of flowers with foliage of different genus, species or variety (cultivar) are, however, permitted so long as produce of the same quality is used and that it is appropriately marked.

The visible part of the unit of presentation must be representative of the entire contents of the unit.

Packaging: Packaging must protect the produce adequately. Paper or other materials in direct contact with the cut flowers must be new. Printed newspaper may, however, be used provided that it is not in direct contact with the flower.

Presentation: Flowers, which are budding or beginning to open, must have reached a uniform state of development in any one variety in any one unit of presentation.

A unit of presentation (bunch, bouquet, box and the like) must consists of 5, 10 or in multiples of 10 pieces. However, this rule does not apply to flowers for which seller and buyer agree expressly to depart from the provisions concerning the number of flowers in a unit of presentation.

Provisions Concerning Marking

The following particulars must accompany the goods either in the form of a label on the package, or in the form of an invoice easily accessible to the control service.

Identification: Packer and/or dispatcher. Name and address or officially accepted code mark.

Nature of produce

(i) Genus

(ii) Variety (cultivar)

(iii) Where appropriate, the word "mixture" (or equivalent term)

Origin of produce

Country or origin and optionally, district where grown or national, regional or local place name.

Commercial Specifications

Class: Size (length code) or minimum and maximum length, number of stems, or number of bunches with the number of stems per bunch. If the number of flowers per unit of presentation does not correspond to the provisions of Section VC. (Presentation), packages must be marked to show the precise composition of the units of presentation contained therein.

Annexure – I

Important Greenhouse Manufacturers in India

Green Field Industries
No 2. 4th Cross, Ullal Main Road, Jnana Bharathi
Bangalore – 560 056, Karnataka
Tel: 080-23213771
Email: ployhouse2001@yahoo.co.in

Indam Seeds
Banashankari-Kengeri Link Road
7th KM, Channasandra Village, South Taluk
Bangalore, Karnataka
Tel: 080-28600356/28602356/28604499
Fax: 080-28602912

Netafim Greenhouses
268-270, GIDC, Manjusar, Savli
Dist. Vadodara – 391 775, Gujarat
Tel: 02667-264601/602, Fax: 02667-264600
Email: response@netafim-india.com

Saveer Biotech Ltd
1442, Wazir Nagar, Kotla Mubarkpur
New Delhi – 110 003
Tel: 011-24634487/24622889/ 24602074
Fax: 011-24620211/24643326
Email: saveer@rediffmail.com, info@saveer.com
Website: www.saveer.com

Sriroz Consultants Pvt. Ltd
B-14, 15, Sant Tukaram Vyapari Sankul
Pradhikaram Corner, Nigdi, Pune – 411 044
Tel: 020-27658989/27657405, Fax: 27656371
E-mail: sriroz@vsnl.com
www:srirozgreenhouse.com

Florance Flora
96 B1 & B2, Ahuja Palace, Richmond Road
Bangalore – 560 025, Karnataka

Annexure – II

Important Irrigation Equipment Manufacturers

EPC Industries Ltd
H-109 MIDC Area Ambad
Nasik – 422 010, Maharashatra
Tel: 91-253-2385179

Finolex Plastro Plasson
Plot No. 399, Urse, Tal. Maval
Dist. Pune – 410 506, Maharashtra
Tel: 02114-23273, 23687,23766/8 Fax: 02114-23770

Jain Irrigation System Ltd
Nain Plastic Park
NH No. 6, Bambhori, PO Box - 72
Jalgaon – 425 001, Maharashtra
Fax: 0257-2258111/22

Alpha Irritech Pvt. Ltd
Plot No. 11, Shri Kumaran Nagar, Kolathur
Chennai – 600 099, Tamil Nadu
Tel: 044-26511818

Harvel Irrigation Pvt. Ltd
301-304, Meghdoot, 94, Nehru Place
New Delhi – 110 019
Tel: 011-26413370

Netafim Irrigation India Pvt. Ltd
268-270, GIDC, Manjusar, Savli
Dist. Vadodara – 391 775, Gujarat
Tel: 02667-264601/602, Fax: 02667-264600
Email: response@netafim-india.com

Plastro Plasson India Ltd
Plot No. 399, Urse
Taluka-Maval
Pune – 410 506, Maharashtra
Fax: 0211-237044

Premier Irrigation Equipment Ltd
Mr. Shrikant Goenka
17, IC, Alipose Road
Kolkata – 700 027, West Bengal
Tel: 033-24795155
Email: response@netafim-india.com

R. S. Productts Pvt. Ltd
A-22, Okhla Industrial Area, Phase-I
New Delhi
Tel: 011-26810413

Annexure – III

Important Rose Breeders and their Web Addresses

Breeder Name	*Web address*	*Specialization*	*Country*
De Ruiter New Roses	www.deruiter.com	Rose Breeders	Netherlands
De Vor Nurseries	www.dewittco.com	Breeder roses for Latin America	USA
Hilverda	www.hilverda.nl	Carnations, roses, alstroemeria, limonium	Netherlands
Interplant	www.interplant.nl	Breeder large, medium, small, spray roses	Netherlands
Jan Spek Roses	www.rozen.com	Breeder Tester of Roses	Netherlands
Kordes Roses	www.Kordes-Rosen.com	Rose breeders	Germany
Lex+	www.lex.nl	Rose breeders	Netherlands
Meilland International	www.meilland.com	Rose breeders	France
NIRP International	www.nirpinternational.com	Rose breeders	France & Italy
NIRP International	www.nirpinternational.com	Breeder roses	France
Olij	www.olijrozen.nl	Rose breeders	Netherlands
Oglevee Ltd	www.oglevee.com	Breeder & virus indexing pelargoniums poinsettia	USA
Olij Rozen	www.olijrozen.nl	Breeding and propagation roses	Netherlands
Preesman	www.preesman.com	Breeder roses and gerbera	Netherlands
PanAmerica Seed	www.panamericanseed.com	Breeder producer bedding, pots, flowers	USA
Penning Freesia	www.xs4all.nl.penbreed	Breeder freesia & amaryllis	Netherlands
Rosen Tantau	www.rosen-tantau.com	Rose breeders	Germany
Schreurs de Kwakel	www.schreurs.nl	Breeder roses	Netherlands
Santamaria	www.santamariacuttings.it	Breeder: Carnation cutting	Italy
Schoneveld Twello	www.schoneveld.nl	Breeder cyclamen primula	Netherlands
Schreurs Gerbera & Roses	www.schreurs.nl	Breeder roses and gerbera	Netherlands
Selecta Klemm	www.selectaklemm.de	Breeder carnations, Impatiens, poinsettia	Germany & Italy
Selecta Westek	www.selectaworld.com	Breeder supplier carnation cuttings	Netherlands
Serres de Oiseme	www.serres-de-oiseme.com	Chrysanthemum, research, cultivation, propagation	France
Terra Nigra	www.terranigra.com	Breeder roses and gerbera	Netherlands
Tantau Rosen	www.rosen-tantau.com	Breeder indoor and outdoor roses	Germany
Terra Nigra	www.flowerweb.nl/terra/	Breeder roses and gerberas	Netherlands
Van Staaveren	www.vst.kvzg.com	Breeder alstroemeria, freesia, limonium	Netherlands
Vegmo Plant	www.ballholland.com	Breeder cut flower from seed	Netherlands

Annexure – IV

Important Fertilizer Manufacturers

Brahmaputra Valley Fertilizer Corporation Ltd
P.O. Parbatpur
Dist. Dibrugarh – 786 623
Assam
Tel: 0374-2500236, Fax: 0374-2500317
Email: hfclnam@sancharnet.in

Chambal Fertilizers and Chemicals Ltd
International Trade Tower
3rd Floor, Block-F, Nehru Place
New Delhi – 110 019
Tel: 011-26462162, 26462163
011-26465218, 26480639
www.uttamkrishi.com

DCM Shriram Consolidated Ltd
5th Floor, Kanchenjunga Building
18, Barakhamba Road
New Delhi – 110 001
Tel: 011-23318261, 23318072, Fax: 011-23316801
Email: dscl@dscl.com
www.dscl.com

Duncans Industries Ltd
(Fertiliser Division)
16, IInd Floor, Siri Fort Marg (Near Sadiq Nagar)
New Delhi – 110 049
Tel: 011-26264008, Fax: 011-26264007
www.duncansfertiliser.com

Godavari Fertilisers & Chemicals Ltd
Beach Road, Kakinada – 533 003
Andhra Pradesh
Tel: 040-23357200/7204, Fax: 040-23354788
Email: hyd1_gfcl@sancharnet.in

Gujarat State Fertilizers & Chemicals Ltd
P.O. Fertilizer Nagar – 391 750
Dist. Vadodara
Gujarat
Tel: 0265-2242451, Fax: 0265-2240966
Email: ho@gsfcltd.com
Website: www.gsfclimited.com

Indo Gulf Fertilisers Ltd. (A unit of Aditya Birla Nuvo Ltd)
P.O. Industrial Area, Jagdishpur
Dist. Sultanpur – 227 817
Uttar Pradesh
Tel: 05361-270032-38, Fax: 05361-270165
Email: igfl@adityabirla.com
Website: www.indo-gulf.com

Indian Farmers and Fertilizers Cooperative Ltd (IFFCO)
34, Nehru Place
New Delhi – 110 019
Tel: 011-26432507, 26432510, Fax: 011-26463833
Email: mdoffice@iffco.nic.in

Juari Fertilizers
Jai Kisaan Bhawan
Zuarinagar
Goa – 403 726
Tel: 0832- 2592180, Fax: 0832- 2555179
Website: www.zuari-chambal.com

Krishak Bharati Co-operative Ltd
A-10, Sector - I, Noida
Gautam Buddh Nagar
Uttar Pradesh – 201 301
Tel: 0120-2534613, Fax: 0120-2537113
Email: cpsingh@kribhco.net
Website: www.kribhco.net

MMTC Ltd
Core I, Scope Complex 7
Institutional Area, Lodhi Road
New Delhi – 110 003
Tel: 011-24362200, Fax: 011-24366675
Website: www.mmtclimited.org
Email: head_dro@mmtclimited.org

Nagarjuna Fertilizers and Chemicals Ltd
Nagarjuna Hills
Punjagutta, Hyderabad – 500 082
Andhra Pradesh
Tel: 40-23357200/7204, Fax: 40-23354788
Email: corp@nagarjunagroup.com
www.nagarjunafertilizers.com

Vardhaman Fertilisers and Seeds Ltd
Pratibha Tower, Third Floor
18A/2B, Pune-Mumbai Road
Wakdewadi
Pune – 411 003
Maharashtra
Tel: 020-5810898, 5814978, 4011121
Fax: 020-4002969
www.vardhamanfertilizers.com

Annexure – V

Important Fungicide, Insecticide/Herbicide Manufacturers

Bayer (India) Ltd
Bayer House, Central Venue
Hiranandani Gardens, Powai, P.B. No. 8420
Mumbai – 400 076, Maharashtra

Central Insecticides & Fertilizers Pvt. Ltd
Yamuna Sadan, 3rd Floor
Saki Vihar Road, Sakinaka
Mumbai – 400 072, Maharashtra
Email: fjt@vsnl.com

Cheminova India Ltd.
(Formerly known as Lupin Agrochemicals India Ltd)
Keshava,7th Floor
Bandra Kurla Complex, Bandra (E)
Mumbai – 400 051, Maharashtra
Email: ndg@cheminova.net

Coromandel Fertilisers Ltd
Pesticides Division [Formerly EID Parry (I) Ltd.]
"Coromandel House", 1-2-10
Sardar Patel Road
Secunderabad – 500 003
Andhra Pradesh
Email: kuppusamyA@cfl.murugappa.com

Coromandel Fertilisers Ltd
(Formerly EID Parry India Ltd.)
Pesticides Division
22-A, T.T.C. Industrial Area
Thane-Belapur Road
Ghansoli P.O.,
Navi Mumbai – 400 701, Maharashtra
Email: ShailaSR@cfl.murugappa.com

Crompton Specialties Pte. Ltd
India Representative
Office Unit No. 701, 7th Floor
Business Point-349, Western Express Highway
Andheri (E), Mumbai – 400 069
Maharashtra
Email: uniroyal@vsnl.com

Crop Growth (India) Pvt. Ltd
1001, (10th Floor), Vikrant Tower
4, Rajendra Place
New Delhi – 110 008
Email: pkjcrop@ndf.vsnl.net.in
pkjcrop@hotmail.com

Cynamid Agro Ltd
C/o. Basf India Ltd
RBC, Mahindra Towers
A Wing, 1st Floor
Dr. G.M. Bhosale Marg, Worli
Mumbai – 400 025, Maharashtra
Email: admin@cyagro.com

Dhanuka Pesticides Ltd
Dhanuka House
Karol Bagh
New Delhi – 110 005
Email: dhanuka@bol.net.in

Elen Crop Science
(Lokenath Agrochemicals)
58/120, Prince Anwar Shah Road
Kolkata – 700 045
West Bengal
Email: agchem@vsnl.net

Excel Crop Care Ltd
184-87, Excel Estate
S.V. Road, Jogeshwari (W)
Mumbai – 400 102, Maharashtra
Email: excelmumbai@excelnd.com

Gharda Chemicals Ltd
5/6, Jer Mansion
W.P. Varde Road
Bandra (W)
Mumbai – 400 050, Maharashtra
Email: ghardaho@gharda.com
agroajit@indiatimes.com

Godrej Agrovet Ltd
Phirojshah Nagar
Eastern Express Highway
Vikhroli (E)
Mumbai – 400 079, Maharashtra
Email: bn.vyas@godrejagrovet.com

Gujarat Agrochem Ltd
B/101, Gayatri Darshan
Thakur Complex, Near SCN Sports Club
Off. Western Express Highway, Kandivali (E)
Mumbai – 400 101
Maharashtra
Email: mail@gujaratagro.com

Gujarat Insecticides Ltd
805/806, GIDC Estate
Ankleshwar – 393 002, Gujarat
Email: gilcdpad1@sancharnet.in

Herbicides (India) Ltd
13-14, Prakash Apartments
5, Ansari Road, Daryaganj
New Delhi – 110 002
Email:dugar@ndf.vsnl.net.in, herbicidesdelhi@rediffmail.com

Hindustan Insecticides Ltd
Core-6, Scope Complex 7
Lodhi Road
New Delhi – 110 003
Email: hilhq@nde.vsnl.net.in

Hindustan Antibiotics Ltd
Pimpri Pune Road
Pimpri
Pune – 411 018, Maharashtra
Email: hapune@pn3.vsnl.net.in

Hindustan Pulverising Mills
209-210, Anupam Bhavan
Azadpur Commercial Complex, Azadpur
Delhi – 110 033
Email: hpmdel@eth.net

Indian Pest Control Co.
Plot No. 1-A, Sector-B
Industrial Area, Govindpura
Bhopal – 462 023
Madhya Pradesh
Email: hpmdel@eth.net

Indofil Chemicals Company
3rd floor, Nirlon House
P.O. Box 9112, Dr. A.B. Road
Worli, Mumbai – 400 025, Maharashtra
Email: mktagro-icc@modi.com, hvschauhan-icc@modi.com

Insecticides (India) Ltd
401-402, Lusa Tower
Azadpur
Delhi – 110 033
Email: info@insecticidesindia.com

Multiplex Agricare Pvt. Ltd
Unit No.180, 1st Main Road, Mahalaxmi Layout Extn.
Bangalore – 560 086, Karnataka
Email: multiplextumkur@yahoo.com
agrkare@sancharnet.in, multiplex@zeeaccess.com

Northern Minerals Ltd
861-862, Dhanuka House
Joshi Road, Karol Bagh
New Delhi – 110 005
Email: rgagarwal@dhanuka.com

Pest Control (India) Ltd
Jagdamba House
Goregaon (E)
Mumbai – 400 063 , Maharashtra
Email: pcilho@vsnl.com, corporate@pcil.co.in

Rallis India Ltd
Apeejay House, 7th Floor
3, Dinshaw Vachha Road
Churchgate
Mumbai – 400 020, Maharashtra
Email: venkat.sohoni@rallis.co.in, akshetty@rallis.co.in

Sudarshan Chemicals Ind. Ltd
(Agro Chemical Divison)
162, Wellesley Road, Sangam Bridge
Pune – 411 001, Maharashtra
Email: sudagro@vsnl.net

Sulphur Mills Ltd
604/605, 349, Business Point 6th Floor
Western Express Highway
Andheri (E)
Mumbai – 400 069, Maharashtra
Email: sml@sulphurmills.com

Sumeeka Exports & Imports Pvt. Ltd
408, Apejay Bldg, 4th Floor
B.S. Marg, Fort
Mumbai – 400 001, Maharashtra
Email: sumeeka@vsnl.com

Syngenta Crop Protection Ltd
14, Royal Insurance Building
3rd Floor, J. Tata Road
Churchgate
Mumbai – 400 020, Maharashtra

United Phosphorus Ltd
Uniphos House, 11th Road
Madhu Park, Khar (W)
Mumbai – 400 052, Maharashtra

Zuari Industries Ltd
Jaikisaan Bhawan
Zuarinagar
Goa – 403 726